Seven Aspects
of God's Grace

Bishop Robert E. Smith, Sr.

D1264488

Seven Aspects of God's Grace

4th Printing 2020

Published By:
Total Outreach for Christ Ministries, Inc.

Cover Design: Sheila Marie Middleton

All scripture quotations are from the Authorized Version of the King James Bible.

Printed in USA by Bethany Press International

ISBN 9-780974-583426

TABLE OF CONTENTS

INTRODUCTION

Apostle Peter wrote in I Peter 4:10 "*As every man hath received the gift, even so minister the same one to another, as good stewards of the manifold grace of God.*" Apostle Paul speaks something of the same nature in Ephesians 4:7 by writing, "*But unto every one of us is given grace according to the measure of the gift of Christ.*" Peter says we have received the Gift and Paul says that the Gift is Christ. John 3:16 says that God gave the Gif, and in chapter one verse fourteen, he says the Gift was "*full of grace and truth.*"

In Titus 2:11 Paul says, "*For the grace of God that bringeth salvation hath appeared to all men.*" II Corinthians 4:6 says, "*For God, who commanded the light to shine out of darkness, hath shined in our hearts, to give the light of the knowledge of the glory of God in the face of Jesus Christ.*" Christ and grace function the same way. Meditate on the definition of grace; **Grace is the divine influence upon the heart and its reflection in the life, including gratitude, acceptance, benefit, and favor**. Christ is God's divine influence working powerfully and bringing about the desired result "*to the praise of the glory of his grace...*" (Ephesians 1:6). Now that we have a better understanding of who and what grace is, we can put our faith in the grace of God.

As diverse and available as grace is, there is yet the danger of it being frustrated and wasted. The frustrating corresponds to faith, and the wasting to works. Paul, in Galatians 2:21 says, "*I do not frustrate the grace of God: for if righteousness come by the law, then Christ is dead in vain.*" In other words, we are made the righteousness of God in Christ (II Corinthians 5:21), thus the righteousness obtained by the keeping of the law (if anyone ever did) still would not be the righteousness that God required for His satisfaction. So, we are told in Romans 5:17 that, "*they which receive abundance of grace and of the gift of righteousness shall reign in life by one, Jesus Christ.*" To think otherwise (faithlessly) is to frustrate the grace of God. Another reference says, "*We then, as workers together with him, beseech you also that ye receive not the grace of God in vain*" (II Corinthians 6:1). When it is time to go to work, and the work is apart from the grace of God's enabling, our work is a waste. In John 15:5b, Jesus said, "*Without me ye can do nothing.*" However, by His grace we can say, "*I can do all things through Christ which strengtheneth me*" (Philippians 4:13).

In this overview of these *Seven Aspects of God's Grace,* we hope to encourage many to give more time to meditating and contemplating the unspeakable gift of God's grace!

CHAPTER 1
The Salvation of Grace

When we were dead in trespasses and sins, walking according to the course of this world, and according to the prince of the power of the air, the Devil, we were in the lust of our flesh, fulfilling the desires of the flesh and of the mind. We were by nature the children of wrath. Then, the grace of God that brings salvation appeared to us. Faith in this grace as a gift saved us from the penalty of sin, the power of sin, and will save us from the presence of sin (Ephesians 2, Romans 6-8). To many, this is too good to be true. Therefore, there is a need to remind some of the meaning of the word grace "the divine influence upon the heart, and its reflection in the life."

Depending upon the biblical administration or the angle in which the gospel was preached to us, we may or may not believe certain truths about God's grace as it relates to salvation, eternal life, and the security of the believer. The idea that "anything good" must be worked for or merited in some way is the by-product of contaminated humanity. Of all the things that we must work for and earn in this life, the one and only thing that cannot be earned, merited, or worked for is the most important of all things, *eternal life*.

After the fall of man in the Garden of Eden, man had to maintain his natural life "in the sweat of his face" (Genesis 3:19). But spiritual life is different! Spiritual life is what God wanted for us from the beginning of time. Anything that we attempt to do to obtain this high life lowers the standard by which it was obtained by Christ. Remember that Christ "*being in agony...prayed more earnestly: and his sweat was as it were great drops of blood falling down to the ground*" (Luke 22:44). We sweat for natural, temporal life, but He sweated in order to bring us into Eternal Life. On the cross, Jesus said, "*It is finished.*" He not only meant that the work of salvation for Eternal Life was finished, but also that "you and I" were finished. When He died, everybody died (II Corinthians 5:14).

There is nothing a dead man can do but receive life from the life giver. This life eternal is a gift of God's "divine influence upon the heart, and its reflection in the life," His Grace.

The Almighty is so serious about this "so great a salvation - so free and prepaid," that anyone who does not receive this Life by faith in His grace will experience the eternal agony of the second death, "the lake of fire" (Revelation 20:14-15, 21:8). The consequence is so severe for not receiving it that it would be unfair of God to expect anything on our behalf except what He himself has provided for us. Apostle Paul is Word-perfect when he says, "*For by grace are ye saved through faith; and that not of yourselves: it is the gift of God: Not of works, lest any man should boast*" (Ephesians 2:8-9). We can rest our case regarding the free gift of grace for the initial experience of salvation. Now let us consider the question of God's gracious sustaining power, which preserves us over time and through life's experiences. It is written:

"*Therefore being justified by faith, we have peace with God through our Lord Jesus Christ: By whom also we have access by faith unto this grace wherein we stand, and rejoice in hope of the glory of God*" (Romans 5:1-2).

And "[*you, the elect*] *kept by the power of God through faith unto salvation ready to be revealed in the last time*" (I Peter 1:5). And again, "*Being confident of this very thing, that he which hath begun a good work in you will perform it until the day of Jesus Christ*" (Philippians 1:6).

Also, the "Much More" ministry of the Lord Jesus:

"*Much more then, being now justified by his blood, we shall be saved from wrath through him... much more, being reconciled, we shall be saved by his life... For if through the offense of one many be dead, much more the grace of God, and the gift by grace, which is by one man, Jesus Christ, hath abounded unto many... much more they which receive abundance of grace and of the gift...*" (Romans 5:9, 10, 15b, 17b).

After a long intense fellowship of leaders in Jerusalem over the question of obtaining, maintaining, and concluding our salvation, Apostle Peter stood up and said, "*But we believe that through the grace of our Lord Jesus Christ we <u>shall</u> be saved, even as they*" (Acts 15:11). To be void of the revelation of God's great salvation by grace is to be insecure and unappreciative of our Lord Jesus Christ. Let us worship our Father in the Spirit and truth of our union life with Christ.

Chapter Two
The Package of Grace

As the word "package" implies, grace brings with it enclosure, which we will intently consider. It is stated in Ephesians 4:7, "*But unto every one of us is given grace according to the measure of the gift of Christ.*" Most evidently, Christ is the total package, inside and out. However, upon the further unwrapping of the grace of our Lord Jesus Christ we find, as it is written in I Timothy 1:14 that, "*…the grace of our Lord was exceeding abundant with faith and love which is in Christ Jesus.*" This statement alone provokes us to lean heavily upon the grace of God. Those of us who are lacking in faith or love are simultaneously lacking in grace. The degree of faith by which we live, and work is dependent on the amount of grace we have or are receiving to live and work. The same applies to love, whether personal or impersonal.

Faith and love are like two thick slices of bread; these two "slices" sandwich a variety of goodies. Notice what Apostle Peter says about this concept:

"*And besides this, giving all diligence, add to your faith virtue; and to virtue knowledge; and to knowledge temperance; and to temperance patience; and to patience godliness; and to godliness brotherly kindness; and to brotherly kindness charity*" (II Peter 1:5-7).

By grace comes the two slices of faith and love; and when "*faith which worketh by love*" (Galatians 5:6) is operating, all of the other attributes mentioned above are functioning.

16

Now we can more clearly see why grace is so important to the whole process. We also understand why Paul received an "exceeding abundant" amount of grace; he needed the faith and love in order to function on the level of the apostolic calling to the Gentile world, yet accept every opportunity to minister to the Jews and care for all of the Churches. Paul said, "*this is a faithful saying, and worthy of all acceptation, that Christ Jesus came into the world to save sinners; of whom 1 am chief*" (I Timothy 1:15). Verse 12 says, "*1 thank Christ Jesus our Lord, who hath enabled me, for that he counted me faithful, putting me into the ministry.*" Think on this: "He enabled me" (His grace); "counted me faithful" (His process); "putting me into the ministry" (His purpose); and "this is a faithful saying" (the messenger was as good as the message). What a package of grace! We as believers should not more or less divorce ourselves from this principle of grace. Paul said that he was "chief of sinners," so there is no doubt that more grace was necessary in his life. Some of us were just as rank in sin.

We can know one another by the grace given with the faith and love, and appreciate the greatness of God in His dealings with man. Paul says:

"For l say, through the grace given unto me, to every man that is among you, not to think of himself more highly than he ought to think; but to think soberly, according as God hath dealt to every man the measure of faith" (Romans 12:3).

"That Christ may dwell in your hearts by faith; that ye, being rooted and grounded in love, May be able to comprehend with all

saints what is the breadth, and length, and depth, and height" (Ephesians 3:17-18).

The package of grace not only provided the slices to sandwich all of the attributes mentioned earlier, but also potentially encompasses all of the people of God as well. If this truth were applied to the church life in the city and to the relationships in the Body of Christ, then we would do well to ask ourselves, "What is the problem?" The answer is Grace. Many are preaching that the primary problem lies in faith or love, but this is not true. Faith and love are automatic in the package of grace.

As we continue on the road to discover the seven aspects of God's grace, I truly believe that our prayers for the grace of God will become much more desperate at the Throne of Grace (Hebrews 4:16).

Chapter Three
The Way of Grace

It is my personal opinion, that in some way we all know that the way to gain the favor of God is through humility of mind and heart. With such a need as we have for the grace of God, it must be clearly understood that it is not the need to know about humility, but rather to be humble. <u>Acting</u> humbly looks too much like uncertainty, fear, paranoia, compromise, or even worse, it looks like <u>true</u> humility.

God's grace carries with it faith and love. Faith and love are the alpha and omega of our spiritual journey and we are yet so far from our destination. So, let's face it: If the by-product of humility is the grace of God, it is concluded that the people of God are not very humble. At least they are not willingly humble.

There are two ways to genuine humility. One is a short cut, the other takes a bit longer, sometimes a lifetime. The short cut is found in Luke 9:23, which says, "*And he said unto them all, if any man will come after me, let him deny himself, and take up his cross daily, and follow me.*" That's simple enough. But Lord, where goest thou? Verse 22 gives clarity to the short cut answer. "*The Son of man must suffer many things, and be rejected of the elders and chief priests and scribes, and be slain, and be raised the third day*". Paul said of Christ, "*And being found in fashion as a man, he humbled himself, and became obedient unto death, even the death of the cross*" (Philippians 2:8). **Humility comes through suffering one way or the other, willingly or forced**. Christ humbled himself and overcame in the school of humanity. What was the lesson? Obedience. Hebrews 5:8 says, "*Though he were a Son, yet learned he obedience by the things which he suffered.*" Suffering that leads to true humility is the result of God's grace applied by the One who knows just what it takes for each and every one of us to be processed.

Christ suffered the transition from glory to poverty, from the earth to the cross; and this all was a result of God's grace.

"*For ye know the grace of our Lord Jesus Christ, that, though he was rich, yet for your sakes he became poor, that ye through his poverty might be rich. Looking unto Jesus the author and finisher of our faith; who for the joy that was set before him endured the cross, despising the shame; and is set down at the right hand of the throne of God*" (II Corinthians 8:9; Hebrews 12:2).

Again, the short cut to humility is self-denial and being mistreated by the elders and chief priests and scribes (religious people and unbelieving believers) that will, by the way, encourage you to pick up your cross and die.

The long way to the grace of God as evidenced by the outworking is rather ugly. Let us take a look at two of God's chosen servants, Moses and Paul. Here, I've inserted excerpts from the experience of Moses given in Acts 7:20-36

"Moses was born, and was exceeding fair, and nourished up in his father's house three months: And when he was cast out, Pharaoh's daughter took him up, and nourished him for her own son. And Moses was learned in all the wisdom of the Egyptians, and was mighty in words and in deeds. And when he was full forty years

*old... Then fled Moses at this saying, and
was a stranger in land of Madian...And
when forty years were expired...this Moses
whom they refused saying, Who made thee a
ruler and a judge? the same did God send to
be a ruler and a deliverer by the hand of the
angel which appeared to him in the bush.
He brought them out.*"

We do not often think of Moses as one who
was learned in all the wisdom of the
Egyptians and mighty in words and in
deeds. His forty years of education and
acquired ability from the world produced a
self-sufficiency that, upon attempting to do
the work of God, resulted in murder and no
deliverance. Humility came with a forty-
year sentence on the backside of the desert.
It took God forty years to get out of Moses
what it took forty years to get into him.
Forty years is a long time for processing true
humility; but I think that it is fair to say that

those servants of God who are going to be used mightily in "word" and in "deeds" will probably mellow after forty years of hard times.

Apostle Paul also had a radical beginning with Christ. It could be called the "apostolic conversion." One would think that after being knocked to the ground, blinded, and humiliated by having to be taken by the hand and led to the city of Damascus, humility would have suddenly settled in. That was not so. One of the most difficult things for God to process out of a man is his confidence in what he thought of himself before his encounter with the God-man, Christ. Years after his conversion, Paul said,".

"...we are the circumcision, which worship God in the spirit, and rejoice in Christ Jesus, and have no confidence in the flesh.

Though l might also have confidence in the flesh. If any other man thinketh that he hath whereof he might trust in the flesh, l more" (Philippians 3:3-4).

He said in II Corinthians 12:11, *"l am become a fool in glorying; ye have compelled me."* Acknowledging the past can make humility a struggle. Because Paul was "circumcised the eighth day, of the stock of Israel, of the tribe of Benjamin, and a Hebrew of the Hebrews, and as touching the law, a Pharisee," there was a possibility of him slipping from "little one" (Paul) back to Saul, the "big one."

It is impossible to live and walk in humility while having secret confidence in race, social status, or religious position. One must either deny himself or be denied the revelation power of God to that same degree.

Apostle James in chapter 4:6-7,10 says:

"*He giveth more grace. Wherefore he saith, God resisteth the proud, but giveth grace to the humble. Submit yourselves therefore to God...Humble yourselves in the sight of the Lord and He shall lift you up.*"

I Peter 5:5-6 says: "*Likewise, ye younger, submit yourselves unto the elder. Yea, all of you be subject one to another, and be clothed with humility: for God resisteth the proud, and giveth grace to the humble. Humble yourselves therefore under the mighty hand of God that He may exalt you in due time.*"

The "mighty hand of God" is the part of Him that cares for His body. His hand is made up of the apostles, prophets, evangelists, and teachers. Space and time will not permit me to go into a complete explanation of His hand or of the value of maintaining the right attitude toward it. So, we will let the scripture sum it up for us in Ephesians 4:11-13:

"*And he gave some, apostles; and some, prophets; and some, evangelists; and some, pastors and teachers; For the perfecting of the saints, for the work of the ministry, for the edifying of the body of Christ: Till we all come in the unity of the faith, and of the knowledge of the Son of God, unto a perfect man, unto the measure of the stature of the fulness of Christ.*"

Remember that God is not missing any of the above gifts to His body. He is working out an environment for humility in order to pour out his grace upon us for the final quest for full expression of Christ and His kingdom.

Chapter Four
The Call of Grace

Grace has a call, an expectation, and a manifestation. Remember that grace is defined as *the divine influence upon the heart, and its reflection in the life.* Grace works from the inside out, giving the motivation and energy to do what God himself is doing. We will discover this as we move along. The calling of grace is so powerful, so awesome, that it takes a revelation from the Almighty to begin to appreciate it. The prayer of Apostle Paul for us is:

"That the God of our Lord Jesus Christ, the Father of glory, may give unto you the spirit of wisdom and revelation in the knowledge of him: The eyes of your understanding

being enlightened; that ye may know what is the hope of his calling" (Ephesians 1:17-18).

The hope of His calling by grace is not a wish that has been reduced to human expectations. The expectation of the call of grace is so far removed from human abilities and achievements that we will never, in this life, perceive the meanings apart from a revelation from the Father of glory.

Here in Galatians 1:15-16, Apostle Paul gives a clear meaning of the call of grace:

"*But when it pleased God, who separated me from my mother's womb, and called me by his grace, to reveal his Son in me, that l might preach him among the heathen; immediately l conferred not with flesh and blood.*"

The call of grace is to "reveal God's Son in us." Notice that there is a separation from the mother's womb and there is a calling by His grace. There is nothing mentioned between the separation and the calling, clearly indicating that there is no significance for any natural history, family pedigree, or even near God experiences called the "Jews' religion." If Christ is to be revealed in us, the natural umbilical cord must be cut and a new life support system must be put in place, the Zoe life of God. Again, this is expressed in Romans 8:28,29, which says, "*...to them who are the called according to his purpose...to be conformed to the image of his Son.*"

The ultimate call of grace is to make God's Son look like the Son in us. Any ministry or message that does not have this objective view is called "another gospel." Notice:

"I marvel that ye are so soon removed from him that called you into the grace of Christ unto another gospel: which is not another; but there be some that trouble you, and would pervert the gospel of Christ" (Galatians 1:6-7).

All that is said and done in life and ministry should result in Christ being revealed and represented as He is. In some cases, we may have difficulty determining how Christ is to be revealed, expressed, or properly represented. This is easily resolved by asking the question, "How was Christ presented to us by His Father?" WE need only "RE-present Him" the same way in word and deed. *What? Speak like Christ and do what He does*? Apart from the call of grace, this is impossible, but by God's grace, I am not discouraged at all, knowing Him as described in II Timothy:

"Who hath saved us, and called us with an holy calling, not according to our works, but according to his own purpose and grace, which was given us in Christ Jesus before the world began, But is now made manifest" (II Timothy 1:9,10a).

Grace has very high demands, and rightly so; for no one can fulfill the call except for the God of all grace speaking and working in us. I Peter 4:10-11 removes any matter by saying:

"As every man hath received the gift, even so minister the same one to another, as good stewards of the manifold grace of God. If any man speak, let him speak as the oracles of God; if any man minister, let him do it as of the ability which God giveth: that God in all things may be glorified through Jesus Christ, to whom, be praise and dominion for ever and ever."

The progressive nature of grace is "grace upon grace" as is written in John 1:16, "*And of his fullness have all we received, and grace for grace.*" To reach the fullness of God is a matter of grace, and this grace comes through the avenue of sufferings.

"*But the God of all grace, who hath called us unto his eternal glory by Christ Jesus, after that ye have suffered a while, make you perfect, stablish, strengthen, settle you*" (I Peter 5:10).

Employ God's grace and stay in the process, for if we bail out of an "ordered life" we forfeit the grace required to live it. Hebrews 12:14-15 makes it clear that we must,

"*Follow peace with all men, and holiness, without which no man shall see the Lord: Looking diligently lest any man fail of the*

34

grace of God; lest any root of bitterness springing up trouble you, and thereby many be defiled."

For Christ to be revealed in us may include the identifying marks of the Lord upon us as well, as declared in Galatians 6:17, "*From henceforth let no man trouble me: for l bear in my body the marks of the Lord Jesus.*" And Colossians 1:24 states:

"*Who now rejoice in my sufferings, for you, and fill up that which is behind of the afflictions of Christ in my flesh for his body's sake, which is the church.*"

This all may seem a little disheartening, but I remind you that" *For even hereunto were ye called: because Christ also suffered for us, leaving us an example, that ye should follow his steps. Forasmuch then as Christ has suffered for us in the flesh, arm yourselves likewise with the same mind: for he that hath suffered in the flesh hath ceased from sin*" (I Peter 2:21, 4:1).

Finally, if Christ is going to be revealed in us, He must first be formed in us. This will not happen without the help of others that have preceded us, and who can say as Paul said to the churches of Galatia, "My little children of whom I travail in birth again until Christ be formed in you" (Galatians 4:19).

Again, the call of grace is very high; it is a call to growth, both in the divine influence and in the knowledge of Christ. It calls for a separated life unto him, and a counting "*...all things but loss for the excellency of the knowledge of Christ Jesus my Lord: for whom I have suffered the loss of all things, and do count them but dung, that I may win Christ. Brethren, I count not myself to have apprehended: but this one thing I do,* *forgetting those things which are behind, and reaching forth unto those things which are before, I press toward the mark for the prize of the high calling of God in Christ Jesus"* (Philippians 3: 8,13-14).

If this is our pursuit, then the next aspect of God's grace is without limits.

Chapter Five
The Extent of Grace

If we have made it through the last couple of aspects of God's grace, it is clear sailing from this point. This is not always easy, but it is very exciting. We have now come to know our Lord in a more intimate way, and have entered into the reality of life, union with Christ, and have established the priority of life-communion with Christ.

Again, we define grace as "the divine influence upon the heart, and its reflection in the life." Now we want to apply its meaning to II Corinthians 9:8 which says, "*And God is able to make all grace abound toward you, that ye, always having all sufficiency in all things, may abound to every good work*." The key words are " "all grace," 'always having," "all sufficiency," and "all things". The extent of grace is always having all of the divine influence upon our hearts, and always having all grace reflected outwardly.

Sufficiency means having as much as is needed in adequate supply. Always includes whenever, wherever, however, whoever, and forever. God is able to make "all grace" abound toward you, because He is, as I Peter 5:10 says,

"The God of all grace, who hath called us into his eternal glory by Christ Jesus, [and] after that ye have suffered a while, [He will] make you perfect, stablish, strengthen, settle you."

In other words, after we have known the way of Grace, which is suffering, God perfects, establishes, and gives us His mighty strength so that we can be steadfast, unmoveable, and always abounding in the work of the Lord (I Corinthians 15:58).

By now, one might ask if this is possible for all of us. Let us check with John for the answer. He says in John 1:16, "*And of this fullness have all we received, and grace for grace.*" By compiling this with what Apostle Paul said in Ephesians 3:19, we get to know the answer: "*And to know the love of Christ, which passeth knowledge, that ye might be filled with all the fullness of God.*" The grace of God is just as available as God Himself. We can have as much of the grace of God as we can have of God. Our hunger for the Lord is the determining factor for His grace.

The writer in Hebrews 12 says, "*Looking unto Jesus the author and finisher of our faith. Looking diligently lest any man fail the grace of God*" (v.2,15). This is literally a "looking away" unto Jesus, a looking with diligence in the same way that we come to Him, believing that He is a rewarder of them that diligently seek Him (Hebrews 11:6). Again in chapter 4:16, he says, "*Let us therefore come boldly unto the throne of grace, that we may obtain mercy, and. find grace to help in time of need.*"

Allow me to give this powerful example of the Grace as it was applied to the Churches of Macedonia in II Corinthians 8:1-7. The chief city was Philippi, with whom Paul had an unusually close relationship. After his arrival there with the apostolic team, he found the people in Philippi to be in a "great trial of affliction" and "deep poverty." However, there was a grace upon them that you don't find in the lives of most people. Paul said,

"For to their power, l bear record, yea, and beyond their power they were willing of themselves; praying us with much intreaty that we would receive the gift..." (v. 3-4a)

Here was a poverty stricken people who were begging. Begging for what? To receive from the apostolic team? No! They were begging the apostolic team to receive from them! Yes, the people that seemed to have nothing but misery were begging someone to take from them what they had to offer. What does a poverty stricken people have to give? The answer is in verse 5, which says, "And this they did, not as we hoped, but first gave their own selves to the Lord, and unto us by the will of God." Now, here is where the extent of grace comes in. Verse 3 says, "...*they were willing of themselves*." Verse 5 says, "...*not as we hoped, but first gave their own selves to the Lord*." These impoverished people received the gospel of

God's grace, and then by grace, in the throat of poverty, begged to give. By grace, the apostolic team went beyond their own expectations to receive the people and whatsoever they had to give in addition to themselves. This is the incorporated grace of our Lord Jesus Christ, "the all grace," as is stated in verse 9: "For ye know the grace of our Lord Jesus Christ, that though he was rich, yet for your sakes he became poor, that ye through his poverty might be rich."

The grace of our Lord Jesus Christ is the clear expression of the extent of Grace. It took this grace for the One who had riches and glory immeasurable by any standard in the universe, to become as poor and despised, as God would allow, and in the context of his poverty, make all of the believing world rich. Remember the words of Apostle Paul in I Corinthians 4:8, "Now ye are full, now ye are rich, ye have reigned as kings without us: and I would to God ye did reign, that we also might reign with you." Again, here is the **extent** of Grace; it brings riches out of poverty. Christ himself had enough in his poverty to make the whole world rich. But the world would never have known had it not been for the extent of God's grace! We too can experience this grace as the churches of Macedonia did. They first abounded unto the riches of their own liberality. Meaning, they were liberal in their poverty, which requires grace.

By the way, based on the example of our Lord Jesus Christ, it requires more grace for one who is rich to give up his treasures in order for the poor to become rich. It requires less grace for the poor to give up themselves and what little they have in order that they might become rich and make others rich by their faith. For this reason, poor people are generally more liberal than rich people are. James 2:5 says:

"Hearken, my beloved brethren, Hath not God chosen the poor of this world rich in faith, and heirs of the kingdom which he hath promised to them that love him?"

This extent of grace so provoked Paul that he wrote to the church at Corinth saying,

"Therefore, as you abound in every thing, in faith, and utterance, and knowledge, and in all diligence, and in your love to us, see that ye abound in this grace also" (II Corinthians 8:7).

What a statement! What a revealing of divine truth! Think of it; one can have the gift of faith, prophecy, speak with tongues and interpret them, operate in the word of knowledge, be a diligent person with

45

personal love, yet not have the **extent of Grace**. May the God of all grace grant this grace unto us!

Chapter Six
The Paradoxical Nature of Grace

A paradox is a statement that seems contrary to common sense yet perhaps is true. And here is a statement made by the Lord to Apostle Paul, "...*my strength is made perfect in weakness*" (II Corinthians 12:9). Not only is this a paradoxical statement, but for the human mind, it can be downright frustrating. Adding insult to the injury of pride is the statement of Paul, which indicates the primary reason he needed grace. Consider his commentary:

"*I will come to visions and revelations of the Lord... He was caught up into paradise, and heard unspeakable words, which is not lawful for a man to utter. Of such an one will I glory...And lest I should be exalted above measure through the abundance of revelations, there was given to me a thorn in the flesh, the messenger of Satan to buffet me, lest l should be exalted above measure"* (II Corinthians 12:1,4,5,7).

We understand the between comments made concerning, "it not being expedient to boast," and referring to the man caught up into paradise in the second person rather than the first, and that he said, *"...though l would desire to glory, l shall not be a fool."* Nevertheless, it was God who gave Paul the visions and revelations. It was the Almighty that caught him up to the third heaven, while knowing all the time that he was giving all of this to a person who had a propensity toward being braggadocios or arrogant. It is as if God was taking advantage of the weakness of this man, and then giving him knowledge and experiences that would later order the horrifically demonic and painful attacks of satan upon his flesh to keep him from expressing his weakness. What a paradox!

Now we are beginning to appreciate the nature of God's grace. In the midst of all of the above, the Lord said, "*My grace is sufficient for thee*," (v.9). I can hear it now, some of us might be saying, "sufficient for thee, not me." After all, who wants this kind of grace in which God takes advantage of our humanity by imposing upon it that which is divine, while putting the undesirable aspect called "the flesh" in check by the unpleasantness of the demonic? Sounds just like Christ to me! Do we remember this:

"*My God, my God, why hast thou forsaken me? Why art thou so far from helping me, and from the my words of my roaring? O God, l cry in the daytime, but thou hearest*

49

not; and in the night season, and am not silent...But l am a worm, and no man; a reproach of men, and despised of the people. All they that see me laugh me to scorn: they shoot out the lip, they shake the head...Many bulls have compassed me: the strong bulls of Bashan have beset me round. They gaped upon me with their mouths, as a ravening and a roaring lion. l am poured out like water, and all my bones are out of joint: my heart is like wax; it is melted in the midst of my bowels. My strength is dried up like a potsherd; and my tongue cleaveth to my jaws; and thou hast brought me into the dust of death. For dogs have compassed me: the assembly of the wicked have enclosed me: They pierced my hands and my feet. l may tell all of my bones: they look and stare upon me...Deliver my soul from the sword; my darling from the power of the dog. Save me from the lion's mouth: for thou hast heard me from the horns of the unicorns" (portions of Psalm 22).

Here is the nature of God's grace in the cross of Christ. II Corinthians 5:21 says of Christ, "*For he hath made him to be sin for us, who knew no sin; that we might be made the righteousness of God in him." Again, "Who his ownself bare our sins in his own body on the tree, that we, being dead to sins should live unto righteousness: by whose stripes ye were healed*" (I Peter 2:24)

The paradoxical nature of God's grace is to convey the life of God through the death of Christ. It is to defeat our enemies by gathering them all to the cross, which includes sin, Satan, the old man, self, and the world. Even the good things are taken out of the way, "*Blotting out the handwriting of ordinances that was against us, which was contrary to us, and took it out*

of the way, nailing it to his cross"
(Colossians 2:14).

Now we return to Paul, who, by the grace of
God, could say,

*"Now rejoice in my sufferings for you, and
fill up that which is behind of the afflictions
of Christ in my flesh for his body's sake,
which is the church: Whereof I am made a
minister, according to the dispensation of
God which is given to me for you, to fulfill
the word of God. If ye have heard of the
dispensation of the grace of God which is
given me to youward...and the grace of
our Lord was exceeding abundant with
faith and love which is in Christ Jesus. This
is a faithful saying and worthy of all
acceptation, that Christ Jesus came into the
world to save sinners; of whom I am chief.
Howbeit for this cause I obtained mercy,
that in me first Jesus Christ might shew*

forth all longsuffering, for a pattern to them which should hereafter believe on him to life everlasting" (Colossians 1:24-25; Ephesians 3:2; I Timothy; 1:14-16).

The nature of God's grace is to work contrary to human strengths and abilities. We see this principle at work in
I Corinthians 1:27- 31

"But God has chosen the foolish things of the world to confound the wise; and God hath chosen the weak things of the world to confound the things which are mighty; and the base things of the world, and the things which are despised hath God chosen, yea, and things, which are not, to bring to naught things that are: that no flesh should glory in his presence. But of him are ye in Christ Jesus, who of God is made unto us wisdom and righteousness, and sanctification, and redemption: that,

according as it is written, he that glorieth, let him glory in the Lord. Most gladly, therefore, will I rather glory in my infirmities, that the power of Christ may rest upon me...for when I am weak, then am I strong" (II Corinthians 12:9-10). That is the paradoxical nature of God's grace!

Chapter Seven
The Sovereignty of Grace

The sovereignty of God's grace here is his supreme power to rule, govern, and make choices as He pleases. He takes counsel from no one but Himself. Ephesians 1:11 says, "*...according to the purpose of Him who worketh all things after the counsel of His own will.*" His own will counsels Him. We have now come to know that grace makes choices. Grace feeds on weakness, inability, the distasteful, and shows itself strong.

We will continue to use Apostle Paul as a pattern. In I Corinthians 15: 9-10 he said,

"*For l am the least of the apostles, that am not meet to be called an apostle, because l persecuted the church of God. But by the grace of God l am what l am: and this grace which was bestowed upon me was not in vain; but l laboured more abundantly than they all: yet not l, but the grace of God which was with me."*

According to Acts chapter 9, God did not ask brother Ananias if Paul was a good candidate for apostle. Ananias's response to Paul's calling was "...*Lord, l have heard by many of this man, how much evil he hath done to thy saints at Jerusalem*" (v.13). The Lord did not ask the church members at Jerusalem what they thought about it either. It is said of them that,

"*When Saul, [Paul] was come to Jerusalem, he assayed to join himself to the disciples: but they were all afraid of him, and believed not that he was a disciple*" (v. 26).

The sovereignty of God's grace transcends all reason, fears and failures to pick the right vessel for the purpose of God. God knows who will appreciate His grace in the long run. In I Corinthians 4:9- 13, Paul speaks of the grace for apostolic ministry:

"For l think that God hath set forth us the apostles last, as it were appointed to death: for we are made a spectacle unto the world, and to angels, and to men. We are fools for Christ's sake, but ye are wise in Christ; we are weak, but ye are strong; ye are honourable, but we are despised. Even unto this present hour we both hunger, and thirst, and are naked, and are buffeted, and have no certain dwellingplace; And labour, working with our hands: being persecuted, we suffer it; Being defamed, we intreat: we are made as the filth of the world, and are the offscouring of all things unto this day."

In other words, he is saying by the grace of God, I am what I am.

Remember, grace uses man's inability as God's opportunity to superimpose His divinity upon our humanity.

"Because the foolishness of God is wiser than men; and the weakness of God is stronger than men. For ye see your calling, brethren, how that not many wise men after the flesh, not many mighty, not many noble are called" (I Corinthians l:25-26).

The sovereignty of grace looks beyond religion and secular humanism (Jews and Greeks) for the religious Jews require a sign and the Greeks seek after wisdom. Grace requires both Jews and Greeks to know Christ, the power, and the wisdom of God (v. 24).

Apostle Paul said, "I am what I am" by grace, and I do what I do by the grace of God. His grace was not in vain. Paul labored more than all of the others. According to Galatians 2:6-9, he says,

"But of these who seemed to be somewhat, (whatsoever they were, it maketh no matter to me: God accepteth no man's person:) for they who seemed to be somewhat in conference added nothing to me: But contrariwise, when they saw that the gospel of the uncircumcision was committed unto me, as the gospel of the circumcision was unto Peter; (For he that wrought effectually in Peter to the apostleship of the circumcision, the same was mighty in me toward the Gentiles:) and when James, Cephas, and John, who seemed to be pillars, perceived the grace that was given unto me, they gave to me and Barnabas the right hands of fellowship."

Sovereignty looks beyond the womb, the good and the bad, and makes choices. It is really not up to us to approve or disapprove, but to discern and take responsibility based upon the grace factor in our own lives. This is brought out in Romans 9:11-14, which says,

"For the children being not yet born, neither having done any good or evil, that the purpose of God according to election might stand, not of works, but of him that calleth; It was said unto her, The elder shall serve the younger. As it is written, Jacob have I loved, but Esau have I hated. What shall we say then? Is there unrighteousness with God? God forbid."

There is so much to be said and experienced of grace that it would take many volumes to convey it all. However, these seven aspects presented serve only an outline and provide some structure for making application of grace wherever needed. This overview is a guide for a more extensive study of the subject of grace.

ABOUT THE AUTHOR

Bishop Robert E. Smith, Sr. D.D., is the founder of Total Outreach for Christ Ministries, Inc. (TOFCM) and Senior Pastor of Word of Outreach Christian Center, Academy and Daycare, headquartered in Little Rock, Arkansas, USA. He and his wife, Dr. Carolyn Ann Smith began their Pastoral Ministry in their two-car-garage where they met on a regular basis with 6 faithful individuals. Total Outreach for Christ has grown into a global ministry which operates a Christian Academy training hundreds of students from pre-K through 12th grade as "Champions for Christ", a school of ministry, a Family Life Development Center, and staff housing on a 16-acre campus in the heart of an urban section of Little Rock. His simple vision for the ministry is "To be a clear voice and working example of God's people on earth. (1 Timothy 4:12; Titus 2:7, 11-15:3:8). Called and gifted to teach, his apostolic calling has lead him to share the message of true biblical reconciliation to overcomers in Asia, Africa, Europe, Latin America, Canada, and the

Caribbean. He has lectured in several places and been a guest on radio and television both in the United States and abroad. He has authored several books for the edification of the Body of Christ including:

- Strong Words About Deception
- 3 Steps to Becoming a Christian
- Revelation on Tithes, Offerings, Giving, and Receiving
- The Prayer of Paul for the Children of God
- Seven Aspects of God's Grace
- The Holy Spirit in You and Upon You
- The New Man
- The Theology of Politics
- I Shall Not Die
- Illuminate, Regulate, and Invigorate, When God's Word Has Free Course